My Re-Birthday Book

THIS IS MY STORY

for adoptees, donor conceived, and people with an NPE, who are misattributed, or who've had a DNA surprise

by

Kara Rubinstein Deyerin

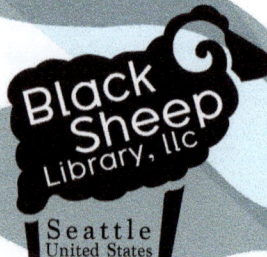

Black Sheep Library, llc

Seattle
United States

Ordering Information
Special discounts are available on quantity purchases by corporations, associations, non-profit organizations, and mental health professionals.

Publisher's Cataloging-in-Publication Data
Kara Rubinstein Deyerin
My Re-Birthday Journal: This is My Story for donor conceived, adoptees, and people with an NPE, who are misattributed, or who've had a DNA surprise

ISBN 978-0-9828336-3-6 (Hardback)
ISBN 978-0-9828336-4-3 (Paperback)

Black Sheep Library, LLC
PO Box 86, Maple Valley, WA 98038 USA
Hello @ BlackSheepLibrary.com

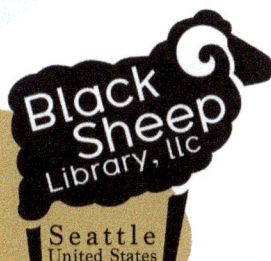

Black
Sheep
Library, llc

Seattle
United States

This journal is dedicated to everyone who is adopted, donor-conceived, or who has experienced a Non-Paternal Event (NPE), misattributed parentage, or a DNA surprise. Your journey, filled with unique challenges and profound self-discovery, is a path marked by resilience and bravery.

Remember that you are not alone. As the seasons shift, bringing change and new growth, so too do the chapters of your life. May you find understanding, support, and a sense of shared experience within these pages as you continue your journey toward self-discovery and connection.

We stand with you, honoring your courage and your ongoing journey towards understanding, acceptance, and renewal.

Right To Know

The nonprofit organization Right to Know is committed to advancing our fundamental human right to know our genetic identity. Since 2019, we have supported individuals impacted by genetic identity issues and the loss of genetic continuity arising from adoption, assisted reproduction, non-paternal events (NPEs), misattributed parentage, or DNA surprises. Through education, mental health initiatives, and advocacy, we foster a deeper understanding of the complex intersection of genetic information, identity, and family dynamics.

This re-birthday journal is designed for individuals who are adopted, donor-conceived, have experienced a Non-Paternal Event (NPE), are misattributed, or had a DNA surprise. You are invited to fill this in as you navigate your journey or afterwards, to bear witness to what you've experienced. We all use different words to talk about our experiences. The language we choose is deeply personal, and here, every word you select to describe your journey is valid and honored. You might refer to the family you grew up with as your adoptive, social, or raising family, and you may or may not have been genetically related to them. Similarly, 'genetic family' could mean DNA, biological, birth, or first family to you.

If you do not have a picture for a specific moment, there is a writing prompt available as an alternative. Above each photo space, there's an area to write a description. At the end of each section, additional pages are provided for writing or adding mementos and photos of your choice. At the end, we have listed some resources to aid in your journey.

May this journal serve as a compassionate companion, guiding you through your unique story and experiences. In documenting this profound and life-changing aspect of your life, it offers a place to reflect, understand, and celebrate the complexities of your identity and family.

The Re-Birthday Journal is divided into four seasons:

Autumn: Reflect on your life before your discovery or search for your genetic family. This is a space to contemplate your childhood, and recount memories, experiences, and perceptions of your early identity and family history.

Winter: This section is dedicated to documenting the emotional roller coaster that accompanies a DNA surprise and the endeavor to identify your genetic family. Here, you can explore how your emotions, perceptions, and relationships have been impacted.

Spring: Detail the process of potentially connecting with genetic relatives, documenting your challenges, successes, and new relationships formed. This is a place for sharing stories and histories.

Summer: Focus on how this journey has affected your sense of self and identity, and how your understanding has changed or developed. It's time to integrate or reconcile your new knowledge with your previous life.

May each season within these pages bring you closer to understanding your own story, as you navigate the ever-changing landscape of identity and kinship with courage, resilience, and hope.

My name today is:

Many seasons ago, a beautiful baby was born into the world

My name at birth or the name I could've had at birth

Autumn

People who grow up in a household being told they are related to their family when they are not, often feel a sense of being different. This can stem from a lack of genetic mirroring, where individuals do not see their own physical and personality traits reflected in their family members. The absence of genetic mirroring can lead to genetic bewilderment.

Genetic bewilderment often arises in individuals who have uncertainties about their genetic heritage, leading to emotional challenges, identity confusion, and questioning of their place in their family. This not only affects self-perception but can also significantly impact relationships and dynamics within the family one grew up in, sometimes leading to a sense of disconnection or altering your feelings of belonging.

Take a moment to reflect on your childhood, your family traditions, and your perceived fit within your family. Think about how these early experiences shaped your understanding of who you are. Consider the roles you played, the expectations placed upon you, and how they aligned, or perhaps misaligned, with your inner sense of self. Acknowledging these nuances can be a vital step in reconciling your past with your present understanding of your identity.

We may mourn not growing up with our genetic relatives. This grief, often disenfranchised, occurs when such emotional turmoil is not openly recognized or validated by society, as these types of losses do not align with conventional expectations or ideals. This grief, often disenfranchised and unseen by many, is an ambiguous loss without clear resolution or closure.

Few people navigate their childhood and younger years without some form of hardship. Life happens bringing various trials, tribulations, and traumas that may resurface when we have a DNA surprise or decide to search for genetic family. It is crucial you have a support system during this time and seek professional help when needed.

After experiencing a DNA surprise or when seeking our genetic family, we often reflect on and reinterpret our childhood experiences. The family we grew up with may no longer seem the same. This is why we begin here—in the family you grew up in, amidst the nostalgic yet introspective ambiance of autumn. It's a season of beauty, but it also carries a bittersweet sense of change.

Autumn

THE FAMILY I GREW UP IN

Autumn teaches us the beauty of letting go. Growth requires release —it's what the trees do.
Ka'ala

Autumn is a time to reflect on the...

- importance of reflecting on childhood roles, family traditions, and one's inner sense of self.
- feeling of being different from growing up in a family without genetic ties.
- experience of disenfranchised grief and ambiguous loss from not growing up with genetic relatives.
- emotional challenges and identity confusion that impact self-perception and family relationships.
- need for a strong support system while dealing with a DNA surprise or during the search for genetic family.

MY Family

photo →
description

Place a 4 x 6 photo or write about who was part of the family you

grew up in. _____

_____

_____

_____

_____

_____

_____

_____

me then...

photo → description

one word that describes you as a child?

Place a 4 x 6 photo of you as a child or write about your favorite thing about you.

_____
_____
_____
_____
_____
_____
_____
_____
_____
_____
_____
_____
_____
_____
_____
_____

As a child, I was..._____
_____
_____
_____
_____
_____

growing up...

photo → description

Place a 4 x 6 photo or write about your favorite childhood home.

_____
_____
_____
_____
_____
_____
_____
_____
_____

I lived in..._____
_____
_____
_____
_____
_____
_____
_____

Here's my family that raised me...

write names or use
2 inch X 2 inch photos

ME

_____

_____

_____

Dad

_____

_____

_____

Mom

_____

_____

_____

Paternal Grandmother

_____

_____

Maternal Grandmother

_____

_____

Paternal Grandfather

_____

_____

Maternal Grandfather

_____

_____

My relationship with my parent(s) was...

_____

_____

_____

_____

_____

_____

_____

_____

_____

_____

_____

_____

_____

_____

_____

_____

_____

_____

_____

_____

_____

_____

_____

MY SIBLINGS I GREW UP WITH

write names or use 2 inch X 2 inch photos

dad   Me   mom

Dad's Child

_____

_____

_____

Mom & Dad's Child

_____

_____

_____

Mom's Child

_____

_____

_____

Dad's Child

_____

_____

_____

Mom & Dad's Child

_____

_____

_____

Mom's Child

_____

_____

_____

Dad's Child

_____

_____

_____

Mom & Dad's Child

_____

_____

_____

Mom's Child

_____

_____

_____

My relationship with my siblings (family) growing up was...

_____
_____
_____
_____
_____
_____
_____
_____
_____
_____
_____
_____
_____
_____
_____
_____
_____
_____
_____
_____
_____

MY COUSINS I GREW UP WITH

About my cousins..._____

_____

_____

_____

_____

_____

_____

_____

Cousin Chart

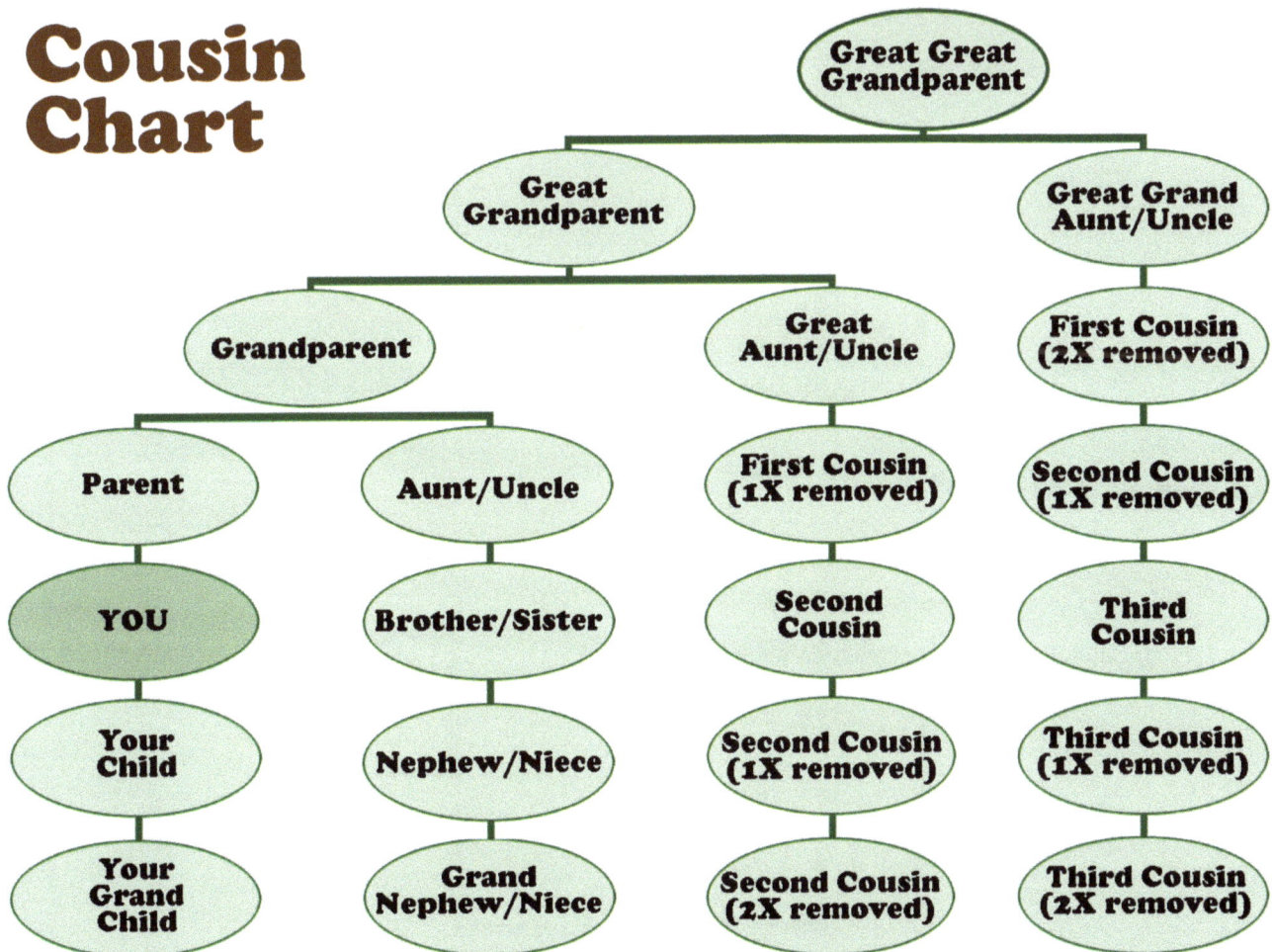

my aunts & uncles

write names or use 2 inch X 2 inch photos

dad's (stepdad) siblings

draw a line to who the child belongs

mom's (stepmom) siblings

my aunt/uncle

_____

_____

aunt/uncle's child

_____

_____

_____

my aunt/uncle

_____

_____

_____

my aunt/uncle

_____

_____

aunt/uncle's child

_____

_____

_____

my aunt/uncle

_____

_____

_____

my aunt/uncle

_____

_____

aunt/uncle's child

_____

_____

_____

my aunt/uncle

_____

_____

Write about your favorite day as a child. Where were you? Who was with you? Why did you choose this day?

_____

_____

_____

_____

_____

_____

_____

_____

_____

_____

_____

_____

_____

_____

_____

_____

_____

_____

_____

**Place a 4 x 6 photo or
write about your first love.**

_____

_____

_____

_____

_____

_____

_____

_____

_____

_____

_____

_____

one word that describes your childhood?

Place a 3 x 5 photo or write your favorite relative.

_____

_____

_____

_____

_____

_____

Some of the family traditions I grew up with include...

_____

_____

_____

_____

_____

_____

_____

_____

_____

_____

photo ⟶
description

Place a 4 x 6 photo or write about your first memory.

_____

_____

_____

_____

_____

_____

_____

_____

_____

Place a 4 x 6 photo or write about your favorite holiday as a child.

_____

_____

_____

_____

_____

_____

_____

_____

Place a 4 x 6 photo or write about a family recipe or your favorite food growing up. _____

_____

_____

_____

_____

_____

_____

_____

HERE'S A COPY OF MY CHILDHOOD BIRTH CERTIFICATE

I always felt like I did or didn't belong in my family because...

_____
_____
_____
_____
_____
_____
_____
_____
_____
_____
_____
_____
_____
_____
_____
_____
_____
_____
_____
_____
_____

Winter

A DNA surprise can turn lives upside down; its ripple effects reverberate through many individuals. Everything you believed to be true may no longer be grounded in fact. You must reevaluate everything you know about yourself and the family you grew up with. Your parentage was misattributed and you discover you have a different genetic family. At this point, you face a decision: Should I search for my genetic family? You find yourself in the same position as an adoptee, a donor-conceived person, or anyone who grew up knowing they were not genetically related to one or both of their parents.

First, you grapple with the falsehoods you were told, the shame you may feel about your origins, or the shame your raising parents might harbor over the circumstances of how you joined the family. Secrets can fester. The way you see yourself, both literally in the mirror and in your personality is now different. The ball is in your court; only you can decide whether your true origins will be public or remain a secret, and how you wish to move forward.

Everything you knew about yourself may have changed: your ethnicity, birth order, relationships with your raising parents and the rest of your family, your name. Take this time to reflect on what steps you need to take to heal.

If you've grown up knowing you were adopted, donor-conceived, have a different genetic parent out there, or had a DNA surprise, deciding to search is a significant step. Most take a direct-to-consumer (DTC) DNA test. AncestryDNA has the largest database among testing companies. During your search, you may contemplate genetic mirroring—how you did or did not recognize yourself in your physical and personality traits within your raising family. As you search, you may think about your ghostkingdom, what it would've been like to grow up with your genetic family.

This is a time in your life when it must be all about you. Setting boundaries is crucial to creating a safe and healthy space for yourself as you process what everything means. Focus on self-care. Engage in activities that bring you joy, whether it's reading, writing, cooking, walking, taking a hot bath, spending time with friends, or watching a movie.

Now we turn to winter, a season for inward thought. It is a time for contemplation, for gathering your strength, and for preparing in its quiet, reflective way for the rebirth of spring. As the cold preserves and quiets the earth, let this period of reflection solidify your resolve and clarify your intentions, equipping you with the inner peace and wisdom needed to embrace the forthcoming journey ahead.

Winter

MY DNA test & identifying my family

"No matter how long the cold, bleak days of winter may continue, winter always turns to spring. This is the law of the universe and the law of life. As long as we hold on to hope, spring is sure to come."
Daisaku Ikeda

Winter is a time to reflect on the...

- profound changes in your understanding of self and family.
- emotional turmoil faced with grappling with untruths about your origins.
- significant decision of whether to search for your genetic family.
- journey of self-discovery, and perhaps imagining your past with your genetic family in your ghostkingdom.
- importance of self-care and setting personal boundaries to create a supportive environment for yourself.

I took a DNA test because

- ☐ health concerns
- ☐ I bought it as a gift and got myself one
- ☐ I thought it would be fun
- ☐ I wanted to know my ethnicity

- ☐ I was doing genealogy research
- ☐ I was looking for family
- ☐ it was a gift from someone
- ☐ _____

circle one

I wish I'd never taken the test

I'd take the test again tomorrow

MY DNA test

I took direct-to-consumer (DTC) DNA tests with the following companies:

- ☐ African Ancestry
- ☐ AfroRoots DNA
- ☐ Ancestry DNA
- ☐ Family Tree DNA
- ☐ Living DNA
- ☐ My Heritage
- ☐ Neubla Genomics
- ☐ Self Decode
- ☐ 23 and Me
- ☐ _____

My DTC DNA results were/were not as expected because...

_____
_____
_____
_____
_____
_____
_____
_____
_____
_____
_____
_____

I received my DTC DNA results on:_____ (date)

I knew/didn't know I had a DNA surprise first thing...

_____
_____
_____
_____
_____
_____
_____
_____

When I received my results I was (where were you)...

_____
_____
_____
_____
_____
_____
_____
_____

After I understood my results, my first thought was...

_____
_____
_____
_____
_____
_____
_____

The first person I told about my DTC DNA results was...

_____
_____
_____
_____
_____
_____
_____

photo → description

Place a 4 x 6 photo or write about how easy/hard it was to understand your results. _____

_____

_____

_____

_____

_____

_____

_____

photo → description

Place a 4 x 6 photo or write about your mood that first week.

_____

_____

_____

_____

_____

_____

_____

_____

After my DTC DNA results, when I looked in the mirror I saw...

_____

_____

_____

_____

_____

_____

_____

_____

_____

_____

_____

_____

_____

_____

_____

_____

_____

_____

_____

_____

_____

_____

Here's how my significant other reacted to my DTC DNA test (or my desire to search):_____

_____

_____

_____

_____

_____

_____

_____

_____

_____

_____

_____

Place a 4 x 6 photo or write how you met your significant other.

photo
description

_____

_____

_____

_____

_____

_____

_____

_____

_____

Place a 4 x 6 photo or write about your child(ren)'s reaction.

_____

_____

_____

_____

_____

_____

_____

_____

I told or plan on telling my child(ren) about my DTC DNA results (or my desire to search), here are my thoughts about this...

_____

_____

_____

_____

_____

_____

_____

_____

_____

_____

THiNGS PeoPle saiD to me...

add your photos, letters, and mementos here

Here's what I'd like to say (or said) to my mom (who raised me)...

_____
_____
_____
_____
_____
_____
_____
_____
_____
_____
_____
_____
_____
_____
_____
_____
_____
_____
_____
_____
_____
_____

Here's what I'd like to say (or said) to my mom (who raised me)...

Place a 3 x 5 photo or write about your mom who raised you.

_____
_____
_____
_____
_____
_____
_____
_____
_____
_____

Place a 3 x 5 photo or write about your dad who raised you.

_____
_____
_____
_____
_____
_____
_____
_____
_____
_____

_____ **(name)**

asked me to keep my DTC DNA results or the fact that I am searching for my family a secret.

Here's what I'd like to say (or said) to my dad (who raised me)...

_____
_____
_____
_____
_____
_____
_____
_____
_____
_____
_____
_____
_____
_____
_____
_____
_____
_____
_____
_____
_____
_____
_____
_____
_____
_____
_____

Place a 4 x 6 photo or write about a secret you've kept.

_____

_____

_____

_____

_____

_____

_____

_____

Who can hold the secret of my origins?

_____

_____

_____

_____

_____

_____

_____

_____

_____

one word that describes your feelings about your DTC DNA test?

THE SONG I LISTENED TO THE MOST:

_____

MY COMFORT FOOD WAS:

_____

I TALKED A LOT IN THE FIRST MONTH TO:

_____

THE FIRST MONTH I DID A LOT OF:

_____

setting my boundaries

guidelines for reasonable and safe ways for others to behave towards you to maintain your well being

What do you need from others to feel safe?

_____
_____
_____
_____
_____
_____
_____
_____
_____
_____
_____
_____
_____
_____
_____
_____
_____
_____
_____

How will you communicate these guidelines to others?

_____
_____
_____
_____
_____
_____
_____
_____
_____
_____
_____
_____
_____
_____
_____
_____
_____
_____
_____

Place a 4 x 6 photo or write about when you asserted a boundary.

_____
_____
_____
_____
_____
_____
_____
_____

Place a 4 x 6 photo or write about when you should have asserted a boundary. _____
_____
_____
_____
_____
_____
_____
_____

Place a 4 x 6 photo or write about your best friend.

_____

_____

_____

_____

_____

_____

_____

_____

My friend's reaction to my DTC DNA test results or my search was...

_____

_____

_____

_____

_____

_____

_____

_____

_____

A peaceful activity for me is...

_____
_____
_____
_____
_____
_____
_____
_____
_____
_____

I do this activity every...

_____
_____
_____
_____
_____
_____
_____
_____
_____
_____

photo ⟶
description

Place a 4 x 6 photo or write about your favorite self care activity.

_____
_____
_____
_____
_____
_____
_____
_____
_____

Place a 3 x 5 photo or write how you looked like your family.

_____
_____
_____
_____
_____
_____
_____
_____
_____
_____
_____

Place a 3 x 5 photo or write about the culture you grew up in.

_____
_____
_____
_____
_____
_____
_____
_____
_____
_____
_____

Paste or draw your ethnicity results from your DTC DNA test

My ethnicity results were or were not a surprise because...

_____
_____
_____
_____
_____
_____
_____
_____
_____
_____
_____
_____
_____
_____
_____
_____
_____
_____
_____
_____
_____

My ethnicity results were or were not a surprise because...

What genetic mirroring did/didn't you receive as a child?

_____
_____
_____
_____
_____
_____
_____
_____

What do you need to move forward and feel whole again?

_____
_____
_____
_____
_____
_____
_____
_____
_____

Positives to searching for my genetic family...

_____
_____
_____
_____
_____
_____
_____
_____
_____
_____
_____

Negatives to searching for my genetic family...

_____
_____
_____
_____
_____
_____
_____
_____
_____
_____
_____

photo ⟶
description

Place a 4 x 6 photo or write about where you'd like to meet your genetic family. _____

_____
_____
_____
_____
_____
_____
_____
_____

Write about your ghostkingdom. How you imagine your genetic family and what it would have been like to grow up with them...

_____

_____

_____

_____

_____

_____

_____

_____

_____

_____

_____

_____

_____

_____

_____

_____

_____

_____

_____

_____

_____

Place a 4 x 6 photo or write about your favorite cultural tradition.

_____

_____

_____

_____

_____

_____

_____

_____

_____

Do you have feelings of being an imposter in your family/ethnicity?

_____

_____

_____

_____

_____

_____

_____

_____

_____

_____

THE FIRST WEEK I CHECKED MY RESULTS

_____ times per day

WHEN I GOT MY TEST RESULTS I HAD:

_____ total DNA matches

It took _____ weeks to identify my genetic family

My top DNA matches were... _____

_____

_____

_____

_____

_____

_____

_____

_____

I identified my genetic family by:

- ☐ myself
- ☐ DNAngels.org
- ☐ my mom/dad
- ☐ a DNA Angel
- ☐ they reached out
- ☐ I hired someone
- ☐ a family friend
- ☐ _____

THE PERSON WHO HELPED ME WAS: _____

photo → description

Place a 4 x 6 photo or write about the person who helped you.

_____

_____

_____

_____

_____

_____

_____

_____

_____

Spring

The decision to venture into a reunion is one of the biggest decisions of your life. This is the time when, despite what your heart is telling you, you must resist the urge to rush mach speed into your new relationships and instead proceed slowly. You need to take time to address past traumas and emotions — you should not ask your new family to help you process these.

Consider why you wish to reach out. What do you hope to gain? Pictures, family and medical history, a relationship? Remember, you've had time to contemplate your discovery and your new family. When you reach out to someone, the revelation is brand new to them. They may need time to process the news. e respectful by giving people the time and space they may need, while also remaining assertive about your own needs.

When you decide to meet for the first time, choose a public, quiet place and set a time limit. Come prepared by practicing with a significant other or a close friend what you want to say and the questions you wish to ask. Even a 'good reunion' can stir up past emotions and prove challenging. Take time to learn about your family's traditions, foods, and customs. You need to gradually build the experiences you missed growing up. There are no shortcuts.

One significant realization is that half, or all, of our medical history might be incorrect, and you may not know your new medical history. Reaching out to your genetic family can help you uncover some missing pieces of this puzzle. It's important to inform your doctor about any new medical information (or the lack thereof) you discover. Additionally, you may need to consider lifestyle adjustments based on this new information.

If you encounter rejection, and this can come from both the family you grew up with and your new genetic family, try to remember it isn't a reflection on you. Rejection often speaks to the circumstances of the person who has decided not to have contact. Take some time to write them a letter; you don't have to send it, but it allows you to express what you need to say. Consider reaching out once a year to update them on your life and inquire about theirs. Alternatively, try connecting with more distant relatives, who may be more receptive.

After the dormant, introspective period of winter, spring heralds a time of awakening and rejuvenation. If you decide to reach out, spring is the season in which you venture forth. It is synonymous with making a fresh start, just as nature initiates a new cycle of life. This season is marked by rapid growth and renewal, offering you the same opportunities.

Spring

My new genetic family & venturing into reunion

"Spring won't let me stay in this house any longer! I must get out and breathe the air deeply again"
Gustav Mahler

Spring is a time to reflect on the...

- motivations for reaching out to genetic relatives while being mindful of their need for time and space to process the new information.
- timing of when to venture into a reunion with the understanding to proceed slowly and to address personal traumas and emotions independently.
- need to emotionally prepare for your first meeting, create boundaries, and practice your conversation.
- importance of understanding and updating one's medical history and making lifestyle adjustments.
- how you will handle rejection from either your raising or new family, recognizing it is not personal.

MY BIGGEST FEAR IS:

_____

MY BIGGEST HOPE IS:

_____

I'D BE CONTENT WITH:

_____

Here's my new genetic family...

write names or use 2 inch X 2 inch photos

ME

_____

_____

_____

Dad (step-dad)

_____

_____

_____

Mom (step-mom)

_____

_____

_____

Paternal Grandmother

_____

_____

Maternal Grandmother

_____

_____

Paternal Grandfather

_____

_____

Maternal Grandfather

_____

_____

The pros and cons of reaching out to my new family are...
Or, if you haven't identified them, how are you feeling about that...

_____

_____

_____

_____

_____

_____

_____

_____

_____

_____

_____

_____

_____

_____

_____

_____

_____

_____

My new Genetic Siblings

write names or use 2 inch X 2 inch photos

dad (stepdad)

mom (stepmom)

Dad's Child

_____
_____
_____

Dad's Child

_____
_____
_____

Mom's Child

_____
_____
_____

Dad's Child

_____
_____
_____

Dad's Child

_____
_____
_____

Mom's Child

_____
_____

Dad's Child

_____
_____
_____

Dad's Child

_____
_____
_____

Mom's Child

_____
_____
_____

Place a 4 x 6 photo or write about your feelings when thinking about reaching out.

_____
_____
_____
_____
_____
_____
_____
_____
_____
_____
_____

photo →
description

One word that describes your feelings about reaching out?

Place a 3 x 5 photo or write who you reached out to first.

_____
_____
_____
_____
_____
_____

My letter/email I sent or would send (or my first conversation) is...

_____
_____
_____
_____
_____
_____
_____
_____
_____
_____
_____
_____
_____
_____
_____
_____
_____
_____
_____
_____
_____

My letter/email I sent or would send (or my first conversation) is...

My first meeting was with (or would be if I could)...

_____
_____
_____
_____
_____
_____
_____
_____
_____

I am (or would be) excited or anxious to meet because...

_____
_____
_____
_____
_____
_____
_____
_____
_____

photo ⟶
description

Place a 4 x 6 photo or write about where you'd like to meet.

_____
_____
_____
_____
_____
_____
_____
_____
_____

I talked to my new genetic relative on: _____ (date)

What I want to tell my new genetic relative is...

_____
_____
_____
_____
_____
_____
_____
_____
_____
_____
_____
_____
_____
_____
_____
_____
_____
_____
_____
_____
_____

Place a 4 x 6 photo or write about the best thing that could happen

at your first meeting. _____

_____

_____

_____

_____

_____

_____

_____

_____

Place a 4 x 6 photo or write about what you think the worst thing

that could happen at your first meeting. _____

_____

_____

_____

_____

_____

_____

_____

_____

I met my new genetic relative on: _____ (date)

I was surprised by my relative's...

_____

_____

_____

_____

_____

_____

_____

I have my relative's...

_____

_____

_____

_____

_____

_____

_____

_____

_____

_____

One thing I have (or think I have) in common is...

_____

_____

_____

_____

_____

_____

_____

One thing that is (or I think would be) different from me

_____

_____

_____

_____

_____

_____

_____

Place a 4 x 6 photo or write what you think you would feel like hugging your relative for the first time. _____

_____

_____

_____

_____

_____

_____

_____

Place a 4 x 6 photo or write if there is anything that would make you uncomfortable about your first meeting. _____

_____

_____

_____

_____

_____

_____

_____

Place a 4 x 6 photo or write about your first impression of your relative.

_____
_____
_____
_____
_____
_____
_____
_____
_____
_____
_____
_____
_____

one word that describes how you feel about meeting your relative?

↓ photo description

Place a 3 x 5 photo or write who else was at the meeting.

_____
_____
_____
_____
_____
_____
_____

Write about meeting your first new genetic relative (if meeting isn't possible, write about how you would imagine it going)...

_____

_____

_____

_____

_____

_____

_____

_____

_____

_____

_____

_____

_____

_____

_____

_____

_____

_____

_____

my new aunts & uncles

write names or use 2 inch X 2 inch photos

dad's (stepdad) siblings

draw a line to who the child belongs

mom's (stepmom) siblings

my aunt/uncle

_____

_____

_____

aunt/uncle's child

_____

_____

_____

my aunt/uncle

_____

_____

_____

my aunt/uncle

_____

_____

_____

aunt/uncle's child

_____

_____

_____

my aunt/uncle

_____

_____

_____

my aunt/uncle

_____

_____

_____

aunt/uncle's child

_____

_____

_____

my aunt/uncle

_____

_____

_____

I learned some members of my family had/have certain medical/mental health concerns and these impact me...

_____

_____

_____

_____

_____

_____

_____

_____

_____

_____

_____

_____

_____

_____

_____

_____

_____

_____

_____

_____

_____

_____

Place a 4 x 6 photo or write about your most recent health issue.

_____
_____
_____
_____
_____
_____
_____
_____

When I told my doctor about my new medical history they...

_____
_____
_____
_____
_____
_____
_____
_____
_____

Place a 4 x 6 photo or write what you learned about your relative.

_____

_____

_____

_____

_____

_____

_____

_____

Place a 3 x 5 photo or write how you're like your family.

_____

_____

_____

_____

_____

_____

_____

_____

_____

Place a 3 x 5 photo or write how you're different from your family.

_____

_____

_____

_____

_____

_____

_____

_____

_____

My first holiday with my family was (or would be)...

_____

_____

_____

_____

_____

_____

_____

_____

_____

_____

_____

photo ⟶
description

Place a 4 x 6 photo or write who was (or who would be) at your

holiday family event. _____

_____

_____

_____

_____

_____

_____

_____

Write about your joys and fears going forward, or if you were rejected consider how this is about their journey and struggles and not a reflection of your value or identity...

_____

_____

_____

_____

_____

_____

_____

_____

_____

_____

_____

_____

_____

_____

_____

_____

_____

(try reaching out to more distant relatives if you've been rejected)

my new cousins

I met my cousin (when & where)...

_____
_____
_____
_____
_____
_____
_____
_____
_____
_____
_____
_____
_____
_____
_____
_____
_____
_____
_____
_____
_____
_____

my cousin

_____
_____
_____

my cousin

_____
_____
_____

my cousin

_____
_____
_____

my cousin

_____
_____
_____

my cousin

_____
_____
_____

my cousin

_____
_____
_____

My first meeting with my cousins was (or would be)...

_____
_____
_____
_____
_____
_____
_____
_____

←→ photo
description

Place a 3 x 5 photo or write which cousin is your favorite.

_____
_____
_____
_____
_____
_____
_____
_____
_____
_____

Place a 3 x 5 photo or write a crazy fact about your family.

_____
_____
_____
_____
_____
_____
_____
_____
_____
_____

add your photos, letters, and mementos here

Summer

You have the opportunity to be who you want to be. Incorporating all this new information into your identity and sense of self is a big task. People often re-examine their past experiences through the new perspective provided by their DTC DNA test results and their newfound genetic family. This is a significant undertaking, but it also presents a chance to develop into the person you aspire to be.

In rebuilding your identity and overcoming any sense of being an impostor you may have, whether in the family and culture you grew up with or your new family and culture, it's important to create new experiences. You get to decide with whom and how you want to approach this journey. Schedule time with the family you grew up with or your new family. Participate in old family traditions or embrace new ones with your genetic family. Take photos. Write down what you learn. Share these experiences with the family you've created—your friends, significant other, children, etc.

When times are challenging, as they very well might be, take a moment to rely on the boundaries you've established and the self-care activities that bring you relaxation and peace. Focus on the small truths you know and build from there. It is these small things that can keep you grounded.

Even when faced with rejection, you can still build family traditions and learn about your new heritage. If possible, talk to your genetic family's friends. Conduct Internet research. Explore the places where your family lived. Look up recipes, movies, music, and books associated with your new family's culture. Again, it's essential to build these experiences one at a time. Soon, you will find comfort and confidence in your new skin.

As you foster your new sense of self, you may consider changing your name or even your birth certificate, though the latter can be challenging to legally do. Changing your name can be an affirmation of your new identity, incorporating your genetic family's name or taking something completely new symbolizing a fresh start.

Summer is a time that often brings nostalgic memories of childhood and past summers, evoking a sense of nostalgia for simpler, carefree times. These memories can be reevaluated and rewoven along with information about your new genetic family into your evolving identity. Summer is the season of natural energy and vitality. It's a time when life feels most active and dynamic, a period of personal growth and coming into one's own.

Summer

MY IDENTITY

"In the depth of winter,
I finally learned that there was
in me an invincible summer.
Albert Camus

Summer is a time to reflect on the...

- opportunity to shape your identity by integrating new information and connections into your sense of self.
- process of creating new experiences and overcoming any feelings of being an impostor.
- importance of focusing on the small things you know to be true to stay grounded.
- building of connections with your new heritage by engaging with books, movies, foods, language...
- affirmation of your identity through choosing a new name or embracing new rituals to start your new chapter.

photo→
description

Place a 4 x 6 photo or write about a moment that captures a personal triumph or a significant turning point in your life.

_____

_____

_____

_____

_____

_____

_____

THINGS THAT ARE TRUE ABOUT ME:

MY first name is:

_____

MY MOTHER is/was:

_____

MY FATHER is/was:

_____

I am:

_____

AND I AM...

☐ adopted
☐ donor conceived
☐ misattributed

☐ had an NPE
☐ had a DNA surprise
☐ _____

Self Discovery Flower

This flower can serve as a reflective tool to explore and visualize the diverse components of your identity, helping you understand how your unique experiences shape who you are. Write a few words in each petal to capture the essence of who you are now or what you aspire to become.

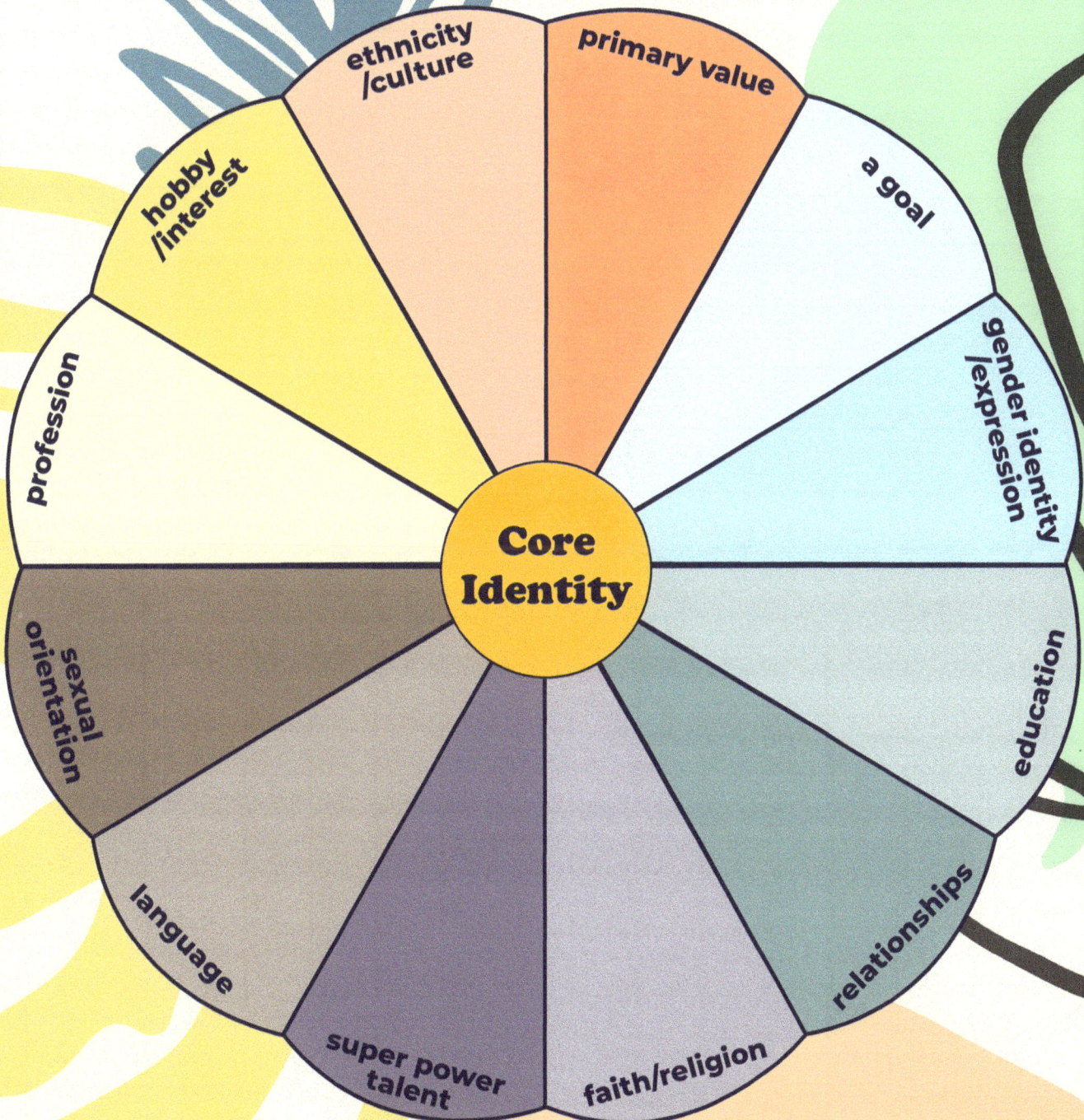

ethnicity/culture

primary value

hobby/interest

a goal

profession

gender identity/expression

Core Identity

sexual orientation

education

language

relationships

super power talent

faith/religion

Now when I look in the mirror I see...

_____

_____

_____

_____

_____

_____

_____

_____

_____

_____

_____

_____

↓ photo
description

Place a 3 x 5 photo or write how you see your features

have changed. _____

_____

_____

_____

_____

Place a 4 x 6 photo or write the first time you practiced a new family tradition. _____

_____

_____

_____

_____

_____

_____

_____

Place a 4 x 6 photo or write your participation in a new tradition.

_____

_____

_____

_____

_____

_____

_____

_____

My family traditions now include (talk about what you've kept from your raising family and incorporated from your new family)...

_____
_____
_____
_____
_____
_____
_____
_____
_____
_____
_____
_____
_____
_____
_____
_____
_____
_____
_____
_____
_____

Place a 4 x 6 photo or write about you and your family today.

_____

_____

_____

_____

_____

_____

_____

_____

Place a 3 x 5 photo or write about who you talk to the most.

_____

_____

_____

_____

_____

_____

_____

_____

_____

Place a 3 x 5 photo or write about who you'd like to see more.

_____

_____

_____

_____

_____

_____

_____

_____

_____

Write a recipe from your new family. If you can't get one, research online and find one you think your family would enjoy...

_____

_____

_____

_____

_____

_____

_____

_____

_____

_____

↓ photo
description

Place a 4 x 6 photo or write your first meal with your new family or what you would want it to be like. _____

_____

_____

_____

_____

_____

_____

_____

I am thinking (or I am not) about changing my name because...

_____
_____
_____
_____
_____
_____
_____
_____
_____

photo →
description

Place a 4 x 6 photo or write about the name change process.

_____
_____
_____
_____
_____
_____
_____
_____

Here's a copy of my Official name change

(or write alternative names you might like to have)

I would/wouldn't like to change my birth certificate because...Or here's how I did... Or how I obtained my original birth certificate...

_____

_____

_____

_____

_____

_____

_____

_____

_____

_____

_____

_____

_____

_____

_____

_____

_____

_____

_____

_____

Here's a copy of my original or new Birth Certificate

(or write what information you wish your birth certificate had on it)

What you would tell your childhood self about your journey?

_____
_____
_____
_____
_____
_____
_____
_____
_____
_____
_____
_____
_____
_____
_____
_____
_____
_____
_____
_____
_____
_____
_____
_____
_____

Me today...

photo → description

Place a 4 x 6 photo of you or write about your new favorite thing about you.

_____
_____
_____
_____
_____
_____
_____
_____
_____
_____
_____
_____
_____

one word that describes you now?

Now I am... _____
_____
_____
_____
_____
_____

add your photos, letters, and mementos here

make a collage of the new you

Resources for People with an NPE

FACEBOOK GROUPS
- Adoptees, NPEs, Donor Conceived & Other Genetic Identity Seekers
- Cross Cultural Connections from a DNA Surprise or MPE
- DNA NPE Friends
- DNA Surprise Support for MPE Family & Friends
- DNA Surprises Support Group
- DNAngels NPE/MPE DC Search & Support
- MPE Jewish Identity and DNA Surprises
- MPE Life: DNA Surprise, NPE, Adoptee, & Donor Conceived (DCP)

DOCUMENTARIES
- Doubting Thomas
- Little White Lie
- Stories We Tell

CONFERENCE & RETREATS
- DNA Surprise Retreat: NPEs, DCP, & Adoptees
- Untangling Our Roots: Annual Conference

PODCASTS/AUDIO
- CutOff Genes
- DNA Surprises
- Everything's Relative with Eve Sturges
- Family Secrets with Dani Shapiro
- Family Twist
- Missing Pieces - NPE Life
- NPE Stories
- Sex, Lies & the Truth
- The Bradley Hall Show
- Weird & Surprising Facts

CHILDREN'S BOOKS
- *A Family Is a Family Is a Family*, Sara O'Leary
- *Where Is My Dad?*, Ambry L Ivy & Taylor Ivy.
- *I Didn't Leave Because of You*, Tyechia White
- *Families Come in Many Forms*, Bella Mei Wong
- *Families, Families, Families*, Suzanne Lang
- *From the Start*, Stephanie Levich & Alana Weiss
- *It's NOT the Stork! A Book about Girls, Boys, Babies, Bodies, Families, and Friends*, Robie H. Harris
- *The Family Book*, Todd Parr

323-TALK MPE
RIGHT TO KNOW
www.RightToKnow.us

DNA Search Help
- DNAngels

BOOKS FOR ADULTS
- *A Broken Tree: How DNA Exposed a Family's Secrets*, Stephen F Anderson
- *Ancestry Discoveries*, Annette L Becklund
- *Black Lotus*, Sil Lai Abrams
- *Exposed by DNA*, KS Hopkins
- *Finding My Roots: A Journal of Discovery & Reunification*, DNAngels
- *Folksong: A Ballad of Death, Discovery, and DNA*, Cory Goodrich
- *How DNA Testing Is Upending Who We Are: The Lost Family*, Libby Copeland
- *I Had My Underwear on the Entire Time*, Michael and Amy Blair
- *Junkyard Girl: A Memoir of Ancestry, Family Secrets, and Second Chances*, Carlyn Montes De Oca
- *My Surprise Family: Find Your Ancestry Story*, Margaret M. Nicholson, PhD
- *NPE: A Story Guide for Unexpected DNA Discoveries*, Leeanne R. Hay
- *Raceless*, Georgina Lawton
- *The Dark Little One*, Shirley Munoz Newson
- *The Milkman's Son*, Randy Lindsay
- *The Stranger in My Genes*, Bill Griffeth
- *The Survivors: A Story of War, Inheritance, and Healing*, Adam P Frankel
- *White Like Her*, Gail Lukasik
- *Who Am I Am*, Dr. Anita Foeman
- *Who Even Am I Anymore*: Eve Sturges, LMFT
- *Who's My Daddy: A Tale of DNA Surprises and Discovery*, Joel Gottfried

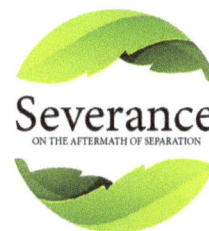

UNTANGLING Our Roots

Not Parent Expected
CANADA

DNA Surprise Retreat

DNAngels

Severance
ON THE AFTERMATH OF SEPARATION

WATERSHED
DNA

NPE FRIENDS
FELLOWSHIP

Resources for DCP

THE DONOR SIBLING REGISTRY
EDUCATING, CONNECTING AND SUPPORTING DONOR FAMILIES

DONOR CONCEPTION NETWORK UK

dcc donor conceived community

U.S. Donor Conceived Council
a voice for donor conceived people

FACEBOOK GROUPS
- Adoptees, NPEs, Donor Conceived & Other Genetic Identity Seekers
- Anonymous US
- DNA for the Donor Conceived
- DNA Identity Surprise & This MPE Life
- Donor Children
- Donor Conceived Offspring, Donors, Parents
- Donor Sibling Registry
- Friends of Donor Conceived Individuals
- Gen Z Donor Conceived People
- International Donor Offspring Alliance
- We Are Donor Conceived
- Worldwide Donor Conceived People Network

DOCUMENTARIES/FILMS
- Anonymous Father's Day
- Baby God
- Donor Unknown
- Father Mother Donor Child
- Filling in the Blanks
- Offspring
- Our Father
- Missed Conceptions
- Sperm Donors Anonymous

PARENTING BOOKS
- *Three Makes Baby*, Jana Rupnow

CONFERENCES & RETREATS
- DNA Surprise Retreat: NPEs, DCP, & Adoptees
- Untangling Our Roots: Annual Conference

BOOKS FOR ADULTS
- *Brave New Humans,* Sarah Dingle
- *Chosen Family,* Kiara Rae Schuh
- *Experiences of Donor Conception: Parents, Offspring & Donors through the Years*, Caroline Lorbach
- *Finding My Roots: A Journal of Discovery & Reunification,* DNAngels
- *Go Ask Your Father: One Man's Obsession with Finding His Origins Through DNA Testing,* Lennard Davis
- *Inheritance: A Memoir of Genealogy, Paternity, and Love*, Dani Shapiro
- *Normal Family: On Truth, Love, and How I Met My 35 Siblings*, Chrysta Bilton
- *Relative Strangers: Family Life, Genes, and Donor Conception*, Peter Nordqvist and Carol Smart
- *Scattered Seeds,* Jacqueline Mroz
- *The Genius Factory,* David Plotz
- *The Ones We Choose,* Julie Clark

Donor Conceived Australia

Severance ON THE AFTERMATH OF SEPARATION

Donor Conception Canada Talk. Support. Learn.

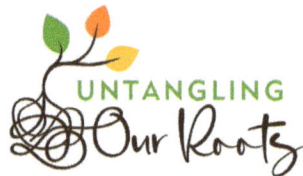

UNTANGLING Our Roots

DNAngels

Right To Know

WATERSHED DNA

- *The Right to Know One's Origins: Assisted Human Reproduction and The Best Interests of Children*, Juliet Guichon, et al.
- *Thicker than Water*, Kerry Washington
- *Triple Helix*, Lauren Burns
- *Uprooted*, Peter J. Boni
- *Who Am I: Experiences of Donor Conception*, Dr. Alexina McWhinnie

CHILDREN'S BOOKS
- *And Tango Makes Three*, by Justin Richardson
- *Building My Family: A Story of Egg Donation & Surrogacy*, Carrie Eichberg, Psy.D.
- *Extra*, Kaeleigh MacDonald
- *Families Come in Many Forms*, Bella Mei Wong
- *From the Start*, Stephanie Levich & Alana Weiss
- *Hope and Will Have a Baby: The Gift of Egg Donation*, Irene Celcer
- *It's NOT the Stork! A Book about Girls, Boys, Babies, Bodies, Families, and Friends,* Robie H. Harris
- *Little Treasure*, Anat Georgy
- *Meeting My Brother*, Jennifer L. Dukoff
- *My Extra Special Leaves*, Jean Wrights
- **Our Story: How We Became A Family Series**, **Nina Barnsley and Stephanie Clarkson**
- *Ready-Made Sweetie: All Mixed Up*, Whitney Williams
- *Sophia's Broken Crayons: A Story of Surrogacy from a Young Child's Perspective*, Crystal Falk
- *The Chicken Who Couldn't Lay Eggs*, Sabine-Julie De Brus
- *The Extra Button*, Jules Blundell
- **Telling and Talking Booklets,** **UK DC Network**
- *Training Wheels; How Did I Get Here*, Chris Barrett and Sally B. Hunter
- **What Makes A Baby,** **by Cory Silverberg**
- *Zach's Safari: A Story about Donor Conceived Kids of Two-Mom Families*, Christy Tyner

PODCASTS/AUDIO
- BioHacked
- Go Ask Your Father
- Half of Us (Half of Me)
- Insemination
- Luke, Who is Your Father?
- Message in a Bottle
- Three Makes Baby
- You Look Like Me

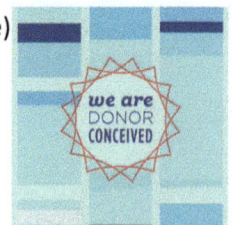

we are DONOR CONCEIVED

Resources for Adoptees

FACEBOOK GROUPS
- Adopted Adults Support Group
- Adoptees in Search of Their Birth Family
- Adoptees Only
- Adoptees Only: Found/Reunion The Next Chapter
- Adoptees Supporting Adoptees
- Adoptees, NPEs, Donor Conceived & Other Genetic Identity Seekers
- Adoption Healing Network
- Adoption Reunion Search and Support Group
- Adoption Search & Support by DNAngels
- Adult Adoptees of Color
- Adult Adoptees Support Group
- Cross Cultural Connections from a DNA Surprise
- DNA Adoptee Research & Reunion
- DNA NPE Friends
- DNA Surprises Support Group
- DNAngels Search & Support – NPE/DC
- Find Birth Parents, Siblings, Adoptees and Family
- Korean Adoptees
- MPE Jewish Identity & DNA Surprises
- MPE Life: DNA Surprise, NPE, Adoptee, & Donor Conceived
- The Adoptee in Me

CONFERENCE & RETREATS
- Adoption Initiative Conference - St. John's University
- Adoption Knowledge Affiliates Conference
- Against Child Trafficking Symposium
- Alliance for the Study of Adoption and Culture Conference
- Celia Center Los Angeles Virtual Adoption Symposium
- Concerned United Birthparents Retreat
- DNA Surprise Retreat: NPEs, DCPs, & Adoptees
- Korean Adoptee Adoptive Family Conference
- Male Adoptee/Alumni Impact Summit
- National Association of Adoptees and Parents Mini Retreats
- Rudd Adoption Research Conference
- Untangling Our Roots Summit

DOCUMENTARIES
- @ghostkingdom
- Adopted: for the Life of Me
- Blank
- Calcutta is My Mother
- Closure
- Dan Rather Presents: Unwanted in America
- Father Unknown
- Lion
- Open Secret
- Philomena

- Reckoning with The Primal Wound
- Secrets & Lies
- Six Word Adoption Memoir Project
- The Girl in the Picture
- The Good Adoptee
- The Lost Child
- The Other Mother: A Moment of Truth
- Three Identical Strangers
- Twinsters
- You Follow: A Search for One's Past

PODCASTS/AUDIO
- Adapted Podcast
- Adoptees On
- Adoption Advocacy
- Adoption Unfiltered
- Black to the Beginning
- Born in June, Raised in April
- Conversations About Adoption
- Dear Adoption
- Jigsaw Queensland
- Luke, Who is Your Father?
- The Adoptee Next Door
- Who Am I Really
- Once Upon a Time In Adopteeland

ORGANIZATIONS
- Adoptee Rights Coalition
- Adoptees Connect
- Adoption Knowledge Affiliates
- Adoption Mosaic
- Adoption Network Cleveland
- Adoption Search Resource Connection (ASRC)
- Celia Center
- Coalition for Truth & Transparency in Adoption (CTTA)
- Concerned United Birthparents (CUB)
- DNAngels
- Male Adoptees
- National Association of Adoptees & Parents
- Right to Know
- Saving Our Sisters
- Watershed DNA

ADOPTIVE PARENT & KINSHIP CARE RESOURCES
- Adoptive and Foster Family Coalition NY
- Adoptive Parents Committee
- Aptitude: A Support Group for Adoptive Parents Facing Adoption's Challenges
- Center for Adoption Support and Education
- Encompass Adoptees
- I am adopted
- Kinship Caregiver Virtual Support Group
- National Center on Adoption and Permanency
- The Honestly Adoption Company
- DVD Series: Adoptive Parent Training

CHILDREN'S BOOKS
- *Adoption Is Both,* Elena S Hall
- *I've Loved You Since Forever,* Juliette C. Bond
- *Sam's Sister,* Juliette C. Bond
- *Surrounded by Love: An Open Adoption Story (Open Adoption Stories),* Allison Olson
- *Tell Me Again About the Night I was Born,* Jamie Lee Curtis
- *The Story of My Open Adoption: A Storybook for Children Adopted at Birth,* Leah Campbell

Concerned United Birthparents

MIDDLE AGE BOOKS

ADOPTION MOSAIC

DNAngels

- *For Black Girls Like Me,* Mariama J. Lockington
- *See No Color,* Shannon Gibney
- *The How and The Why,* Cynthia Hand
- *The Inexplicable Logic of My Life,* Benjamin Alire Sáenz
- *The King of Slippery Falls,* Sid Hite
- *The Length of a String,* Elissa Brent Weissman

BOOKS FOR ADULT ADOPTEES
- *A Fire is Coming,* Emma Stevens
- *Adoption Unfiltered: Revelations from Adoptees, Birth Parents, Adoptive Parents, and Allies,* Sara Easterly, Kelsey Vander Vliet Ranyard, and Lori Holden
- *Austerlitz,* W.G. Sebald
- *Akin to the Truth / After the Truth,* Paige Strickland
- *All You Can Ever Know,* Nicole Chung

- *American Baby,* Gabrielle Glaser
- *Birthmark,* Loraine Dusky
- *Coming Home to Self: The Adopted Children Grows Up,* Nancy Verrier
- *Finding Karen Black: Roots Become Wings,* Diane Bay
- *Forbidden Roots,* Fred Nicora
- *Growing Up Black in White,* Kevin Hofmann
- *Hole in My Heart,* Loraine Dusky
- *I'll Always Carry You: A Mother's Story of Adoption..,* Linda Franklin
- *In Their Own Voices: Transracial Adoptees Tell Their Stories,* Rita J. Simon and Rhonda M. Roorda
- *No Names to be Given,* Julia Brewer Daily
- *Parallel Universes: The Story of Rebirth,* David Bohl
- *Recycled,* Jack F Rocco MD
- *Second Choice: Growing Up Adopted,* Robert Andersen
- *Tapioca Fire,* Suzanne Gilbert and Michelle Kriegman
- *Thank God I Was Adopted: 'Cause DNA is No Joke!,* Pekitta Tynes
- *The Adoptee Survival Guide,* Lynn Grubb
- *The Child Catchers,* Kathryn Joyce
- *The Family of Adoption,* Dr. Joyce Maguire Pavao
- *The Girls Who Went Away,* Ann Fessler
- *The Goodbye Baby: Adoptee Diaries,* Elaine Pinkerton
- *The Lies That Bind,* Laureen Pittman
- *The Other Mother,* Carol Schaefer
- *The Primal Wound,* Nancy Verrier
- *The Truth So Far,* Jennifer Dyan Ghoston
- *Uprooted,* Peter J. Boni
- *You Don't Know How Lucky You Are,* Rudy Owens
- *You Don't Look Adopted,* Anne Hefron
- *You Should Be Grateful,* Angela Tucker
- *You'll Forget This Ever Happened,* Laura Engel
- *Who Am I Really,* Damon Davis
- *Why Be Happy When You Can Be Normal?,* Jeanette Winterson